ZANY, BRAINY ANIMALS

HOW ANIMALS LEARN

DR. ASHLEY WARD AND ANDY ROWLAND

PowerKiDS press

Published in 2026
by The Rosen Publishing Group, Inc.
2544 Clinton Street, Buffalo, NY 14224

First published in Great Britain in 2024 by Wayland

Editor: Elise Short
Designer: Rachel Lawston

Cataloging-in-Publication Data

Names: Ward, Ashley, author. | Rowland, Andy, 1962-, illustrator.
Title: How animals learn / by Dr. Ashley Ward, illustrated by Andy Rowland.
Description: Buffalo, NY : PowerKids Press, 2026. | Series: Zany, brainy animals | Includes glossary and index.
Identifiers: ISBN 9781499454185 (pbk.) | ISBN 9781499454192 (library bound) | ISBN 9781499454208 (ebook)
Subjects: LCSH: Animal intelligence--Juvenile literature. | Animal behavior--Juvenile literature.
Classification: LCC QL785.W373 2026 | DDC 591.5'13--dc23

Manufactured in the United States of America
CPSIA Compliance Information: Batch #CSPK26. For further information contact Rosen Publishing at 1-800-237-9932.

Find us on

Picture credits:
Alamy: Biosphotos 19.
Shutterstock:Karel Bartik 22, Willyam Bradberry 28, Steve Cymro 6, Cynoclub 14, EcoPrint 18, E.O. 24, Tobias Hauke 3, 9b, Eric Isselee 15,17t, 26, 27b, Rosa Jay 5br, 27t, Oksana Kuzmina 29b, Chris Lawrence Travel 2, 23, Sean Lema 12, Sardo Michael 25, Nagel Photography 5bl, Denis Nata 4, Phant 10, rujithai 7t, 7c, 7cb, 7b, Seb c'est bien 21b, Michael Siluk 8t, Arnau Soler 16t, Tsekhmister 11, Vojce 13, wildestanimal 20.

CONTENTS

HOW DO WE LEARN?

If you've ever met a baby, you'll know that it's pretty difficult to have a conversation with them. There you are with all your words, and perhaps with a joke or two to tell, and there's the baby just saying **"GOO"** or **"GA"** and not laughing at those jokes. They're a tough audience for any comedian.

The reason, of course, is that babies have to learn to talk. In fact, there's a whole lot of things that they'll have learn. The same is true for most animals: they're born knowing very little. To equip themselves for the challenges of life, they have to learn.

This book is all about learning, and all of the amazing ways in which animals develop the skills they need to **THRIVE**.

TALES FROM THE LAB

Understanding animal behavior is not an easy task. First, scientists watch animals living their life. That's how they get their ideas. Then they test these ideas by running experiments. If they're lucky, they'll find out something that no one has ever known about animals, which is the most exciting thing possible! In this book, you'll find many amazing discoveries about how animals learn.

BORN KNOWING

Animals might not know much at first, but that's not the same as saying they know nothing. Lots of newborn animals understand what to do right from the start.

Female turtles lay their eggs at the bottom of deep pits that they dig in sandy beaches. A few weeks later, when the baby turtles hatch, they know that they have to burrow **UPWARDS** to reach the surface.

Next, they have to reach the sea to begin their ocean existence. To find the sea, they know that they should head **DOWNHILL** (because the sea is always downhill from their nests). They also know to head **TOWARDS LIGHT** because turtles usually hatch at night, and the glint of the moonlight off the sea tells them where they need to be.

The turtle hatchlings aren't taught to do this. They just know, thanks to a series of simple instructions written into their genes, allowing them to make a good start in life.

TALES FROM THE LAB

Because there is safety in numbers, baby turtles all hatch and leave the nest at the same time. But how do they do this? To find out, a team of scientists buried microphones and recording devices in turtle nests. They discovered that the turtles chirp at one another from inside their eggs to coordinate hatching!

LEARNING EARLY

Amazingly, animals can learn some things before they're even born. For instance, crickets–the jumping insects you might hear chirping in the fields in summer–are left instructions by their mother that help prepare them for life after they hatch.

This happens when the mother has faced some **SCARY PREDATOR**, such as a spider, while she's carrying her eggs. Before she lays those eggs, she sends her unborn offspring a chemical message that tells them: **"BEWARE! SPIDER DANGER!"**

Even though their mother doesn't hang around to take care of them once they hatch, the young crickets emerge from their eggs pre-warned that there are spiders lurking. As a result, they're much more cautious than the offspring of mother crickets that haven't sent their kids a spider warning.

TALES FROM THE LAB

When scientists wanted to test this by showing spiders to cricket moms-to-be, they wanted to make sure that the spiders couldn't actually eat the crickets. How did they do this? They put little blobs of wax on the spiders' fangs, stopping them from munching the crickets.

WHO'S THE MOMMY?

Lots of young animals get support from their parents, but how do they know who their parents are? Some animals, especially birds, use a simple rule, known as **IMPRINTING**, to work out who they should turn to. The first large animal they see after they hatch—that's their mom.

You might have seen a procession of ducklings following their mother as she walks down a riverbank into the water. Each of those ducklings formed a close attachment to her right after they hatched. From then on, until they're grown-up enough to look after themselves, they'll stick close by her side, walking along that riverbank and swimming in the river.

Sometimes, however, young birds can imprint on the **WRONG ANIMAL**. This happens when eggs are hatched away from their parents, by people. When the chicks emerge, they take one look at those people and decide: that is Mom!

TALES FROM THE LAB

One of the great early researchers in animal behavior, Konrad Lorenz, managed to acquire an instant family of baby geese after hatching them. The geese followed Konrad around, as if he was their parent, and he had to teach them to swim and to fly, just like their mother would have done.

GETTING USED TO THINGS

Learning isn't a process of just gathering information. It's also about knowing which bits of information are important, and which aren't.

This kind of learning is known as habituation, and it was first studied in a strange kind of mollusk called a sea hare. Researchers wondered whether sea hares, which have only the tiniest brains, could learn. To find out, they did a simple experiment. As a sea hare crawled along, they **POKED IT WITH A STICK.**

No one likes being poked with a stick no matter how gently, and sea hares are no exception. They responded by curling up in a defensive ball. After a while, each hare seemed to decide that the coast was clear and that they could uncurl to get on with their day.

Unfortunately, when this happened the researchers would poke them again, and again the hare would curl up. But this time they didn't curl up for as long. This process carried on for a while until the sea hares realized that the gentle poke didn't cause them harm and **WASN'T DANGEROUS**. Simple though they are, they learned that this was something they could ignore.

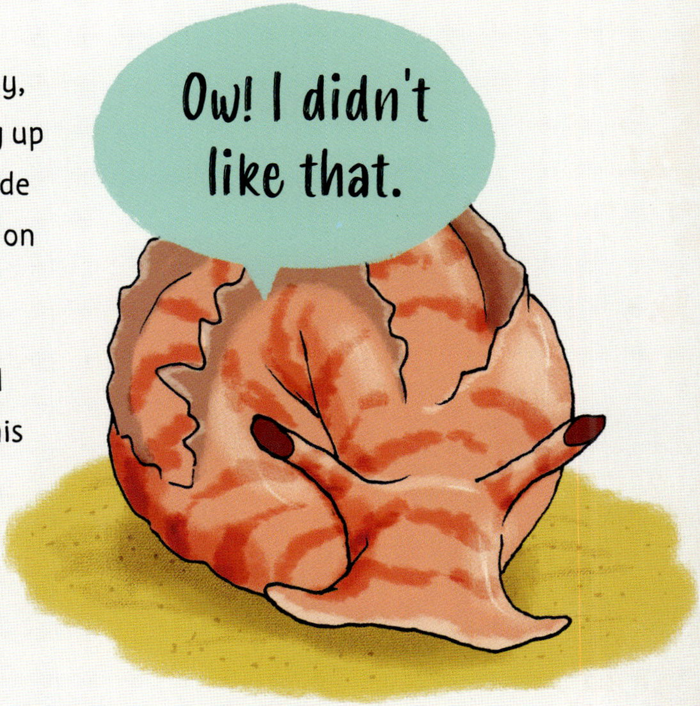

Curled-up sea hare

MAKING CONNECTIONS

Animals make connections between events in their lives, and learn that actions have consequences. One of the most important ways that animals learn is by **CONNECTING DIFFERENT EVENTS OR SIGNALS.**

Just over 100 years ago, a Russian man called Ivan Pavlov showed how this worked. When you give an animal some food, it'll start to salivate, which means its mouth fills with saliva. The saliva helps to moisten the food and makes it easier for them to eat.

What Ivan found was that if he rang a bell shortly before he gave his dogs some food each day, they soon realized that the bell meant food was on its way and they started to salivate as soon as they heard the ringing.

Learning how different things connect allows animals to **UNDERSTAND** the jumble of sights, sounds, and smells that they experience every day. By piecing things together they can **MAKE SENSE** of their world.

The connections that animals make mean that we can train them by rewarding certain behaviors. They're quick learners too. Service dogs can be trained to look out for dangers for their owners, fetch medicines, and even bring snacks from the fridge!

COPY CATS—AND BIRDS

Watching someone else do something is a great way to learn.

At the beginning of the 1900s, the British population of little birds known as blue tits was facing a long, cold, and hungry winter. But then one bird in a southern coast town came up with a **BRILLIANT IDEA**.

Every morning, bottles of milk were delivered to the doorsteps of houses all over the country. The bottle tops were covered with wax paper to protect them. But this one bird worked out a way to poke holes in the lids to get a drink of the rich layer of cream at the top of the milk.

Soon, other hungry blue tits began copying that first bird and before long, the idea had spread throughout the whole country. People tried to stop the birds by using different lids on the milk bottles, but each time the birds **SOLVED THE PROBLEM**. It just took one smart bird to figure it out so the rest could copy.

TALES FROM THE LAB

To better understand how blue tits learned from each other, a team of scientists In Oxford taught four groups of great tits from five different populations to get food out of puzzle boxes. When they were released back into their local woods, puzzle boxes had been set up. The scientists observed that the birds taught their friends to open the boxes!

LESSONS IN LIFE

Lots of things in life are difficult and sometimes young animals need to be shown how to do them by more experienced adults.

Not many things are as tricky to deal with as scorpions, yet they form an important part of the diet of small, desert-living mammals known as meerkats. When they're cornered, scorpions can fight back using their crab-like pincers, and worse still, the venomous sting in their tail.

With such dangerous prey on the menu, adult meerkats have to give their youngsters a step-by-step guide to dealing with angry scorpions without getting hurt.

A skillful meerkat can rush in to deliver a quick bite to the pincers and the sting. This puts the scorpion's weapons **OUT OF ACTION**, allowing the young meerkat to feed safely. It's a lesson all young meerkats need to learn, and it's their elders who show them.

Most of the time, youngsters are taught by older, experienced animals. But this isn't always so. In some species of crows, scientists have shown that the youngsters are just as likely to teach their elders as the other way around.

WHALE SONGS

Sometimes, a particular behavior can spread right through a population of animals. One of the most amazing examples of this comes from humpback whales.

Each year, the whales travel to warm waters to breed, and when they do, the males sing to attract a mate. Each whale could make up their own song, but they don't. Instead, they seem to listen to one another and think **"HMM, THAT'S CATCHY!"** and then copy it.

Often, they make the song their own by adding little bits in, but what happens then is that the other whales copy those new bits for themselves. The result is that all the whales in an area end up singing the same song.

But every so often, one whale gets tired of the old music and comes up with a completely different tune. If it's a really good song, and if the audience of whales in the area love it, there's a **REVOLUTION**. All of the whales learn the new song, and that's the only one they'll use for a few years.

TALES FROM THE LAB

Once, while studying humpbacks, a scientist was lucky enough to find a singing whale. He sang with his head down and his tail up toward the surface, and he held his fins outwards, like the arms of a singer on stage. And whales are LOUD! They're louder even than the sound of a plane taking off, and their song makes your whole body shake!

CUNNING CREATURES

Just like us, animals face really complicated challenges and they have to think hard about how to solve them. This is known as **INSIGHT LEARNING**, and it's something that only the **CLEVEREST ANIMALS** can do.

Chimpanzees and dolphins are among the smartest creatures out there, but one of the best examples of insight learning comes from a bird known as a heron.

Herons normally catch their dinner–a nice, tasty fish–by standing very still at the water's edge and waiting for the fish to swim by. Then the herons grab their prey with their beak and gulp it down.

The problem is that they might have to stick around for awhile waiting for a fish, and some herons aren't good at being patient. So they came up with a **SMARTER WAY OF FISHING**. Watching people feed bread to ducks, the herons noticed that fish like bread too. So herons collect the bread and float it on the water just in front of them.

The fish smell the bread and hurry over to check it out. When they do, the heron is waiting!

TALES FROM THE LAB

Scientists used to think animal intelligence was down to how big their brains are, but that doesn't tell the whole story. The clever herons in this story have tiny brains. In fact, studies have proved birds like crows and ravens are in some ways just as smart as chimps and gorillas (see page 25). We clearly have much more to learn about animal intelligence.

HOW GOOD ARE ANIMALS' MEMORIES?

Some animals have **AMAZING** memories.

There's a little fish, known as a frillfin goby, that lives in tropical rock pools. If danger threatens, like when it's being chased by a seagull or a crab, the goby has a **NEAT TRICK** to get out of trouble. Whenever something scares it, the goby jumps from its pool to another nearby one.

That's impressive on its own, but to do this, the frillfin goby must make a mental map and memorize the **EXACT POSITION** of every rock pool on the shore. It must do this at high tide, because once the tide goes out, it can't look to see where each pool is. The goby knows it has to remember where they all are. If it jumps and misses a pool, it'll end up out of water and in real trouble. The amazing thing is, the goby almost never misses!

TALES FROM THE LAB

Scientists working with chimps have shown that these apes have even better memories than we do. Using computerized tests that examine their ability to remember a series of numbers that flash onto a screen, young chimps do better than people about 90 percent of the time.

WHO'S WHO?

Just like us, animals make friends with each other. An important part of that, of course, is that they need to be able to tell different individuals apart. The way that humans often do this is through **FACIAL RECOGNITION**. We can use this skill to pick out our friends from among a crowd of strangers.

Animals use all sorts of different ways to recognize one another and some, like us, use faces.

To us, most sheep look pretty much exactly alike, but for sheep it's a very different matter. They can recognize at least 50 other sheep, just from pictures of their faces.

Even more amazingly, while we struggle to tell sheep apart by looking at their faces, sheep are pretty good at identifying different people. They're able to recognize familiar people from pictures of their faces, and they **NEVER FORGET** someone who's kind to them.

TALES FROM THE LAB

To test whether sheep could recognize people's faces, researchers gave them pictures of famous people to learn. One picture they used was that of Emma Watson, who played Hermione in the *Harry Potter* films.

LEARNING LANGUAGES

For most of history, people assumed that animals don't really have languages, or that if they did, they're really simple, consisting of just a few squeals or grunts. Now we know that this isn't true, and that lots of animals learn languages, **JUST LIKE US**.

Some animals even have their own name. Dolphins, for instance, each learn a unique kind of whistle that they use to identify themselves to other dolphins.

Animals have even been taught human languages. One famous example is Koko the gorilla, who learned to **COMMUNICATE WITH PEOPLE** using **SIGN LANGUAGE**.

Koko had a pet cat that she called "All Ball." Once, after Koko was perhaps feeling embarrassed after making a terrible mess of her enclosure, she used sign language to tell a fib. When her keepers asked Koko why there was such a mess, she replied: "Cat did it." Naughty Koko!

TALES FROM THE LAB

Nowadays, scientists have switched from trying to teach animals like Koko to speak human languages. Using advanced technology, we're listening to the conversations of creatures such as elephants and dolphins, and we're beginning to understand what they're talking about.

GLOSSARY

Attachment the bond or close connection between a young animal and its mother or whoever looks after it

Behavior the way in which a person or animal acts

Breed to make babies

Burrow to dig

Consequence a result of a particular action or situation

Genes the building blocks of material that carry all the information about how a living thing will look and function

Hatchling a young bird or animal that has recently come out of its egg

Mammal a warm-blooded animal with fur or hair on its skin and a skeleton inside its body. Mammal mothers produce milk to feed their babies

Mate one of a pair of animals that have babies together

Moisten to make slightly wet

Mollusk any animal that has a soft body, no skeleton, and is often covered with a shell. Many mollusks live in water. Snails and octopuses are mollusks.

Offspring the child or young of a particular living thing

Population all the people or animals of a particular type or group that live in one country, area or place

Predator an animal that hunts other animals for food

Prey an animal that is hunted or caught for food, usually by another animal

Rock pool a small area of seawater contained by the rocks around it

Service dog a dog trained to help people with disabilities or people with medical conditions in lots of different ways

FURTHER INFORMATION

Books

Science-ology!: Zoology by Anna Claybourne (PowerKids Presss, 2026)

Smartest Animals by Lily Austen (Jump!, 2025)

Super-Smart Animals by Joanna Mattern (Top Rank, 2025)

Websites

Explore zoology, the study of animals through articles and games:
www.amnh.org/explore/ology/zoology

Investigate all kinds of animals here:
https://kids.nationalgeographic.com/animals

INDEX